MW01538588

ABOUT THIS BOOK

Starting school is a time of change for both parents and children. It's an exciting time for children, and perhaps an emotional one for parents as the school and the teacher come into your lives. It is sometimes a difficult period, but there is much you can do to help your child cope with an experience which will provide many new friends, broaden horizons, and launch him or her on the road to independence.

The more familiar your child is with the school situation before the first day, the better he or she will cope. This book introduces some of the situations your child will meet. Read through the book together and discuss anything which worries your child. Seemingly tiny things, like knowing where to hang his or her coat, are important to a young child. You will need to take your child to visit the school before the first day so that he or she can see what it is like and allay any fears. Build up your child's confidence, encourage sharing, and teach him or her those little personal skills, such as dressing, which will help develop self-assurance and independence.

James Fitzsimmons
(Cert. Ed., Head of Infants)

Rhona Whiteford
(B.A. (Open), Cert. Ed., former Head of Infants)

starting school

written by
James Fitzsimmons and
Rhona Whiteford

illustrated by Terry Burton

Filmset in Nelson Teaching Alphabet
by kind permission of
Thomas Nelson and Son Ltd.

Copyright © 1990 by World International Publishing Limited.
All rights reserved.
Published in Great Britain by World International Publishing Limited,
An Egmont Company, Egmont House, P.O. Box 111, Great Ducie Street,
Manchester M60 3BL.
Printed in DDR.
ISBN 0 7235 4118 3

A CIP catalogue record for this book is available from the British Library.

Visiting your new school

You will soon be old enough to go to school.
Some of your friends may be there already.

There are exciting things to do and
children to play with.
Have you visited your school yet?

Getting ready

It's fun getting ready for your first day at school.

Off you go!
Wave goodbye.
See you later!
And off you go into school with the
other children.

Welcome to school

Your new teacher will look after you
and show you your own special
coat peg.

Have a good look around.
You will soon find out where
everything is.

In the classroom

You will have new things to do
each day.

Where would you like to play in this classroom?

Playtime

Your class and all the other classes
will go outside to play in
the playground.

Do you like to run around outside with your friends?

Assembly

Every day all the children and the teachers meet together in the big hall.

P.E. and games

Sometimes you will go into the hall to play on the big toys.

Or maybe you will play games with
the small toys.
Which would you like best?

Learning how to read and write

Books are fun to read and you will love learning how to write.

Have you got books at home?

Learning about maths and science

You will learn lots of interesting things to do with numbers.

You will also find out how things are
made and how they work.

Out and about

Perhaps you will go out of school with
your teacher and your friends on
a trip.

Do you like to go out exploring?

Time for music

There will be instruments to play
at school.
You can make wonderful noises
with them.

Story time

Sometimes you will be very quiet.
Your teacher will read a story
just before home time.

Home time

When it is time to go home Mum or
Dad will be waiting for you.

Goodbye!
See you tomorrow, everyone.